FINDING A VOICE:
Women's Fight for Equality in U.S. Society

WOMEN'S RIGHTS ON THE FRONTIER

THERESE DeANGELIS

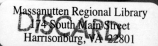

FINDING A VOICE:

Women's Fight for Equality in U.S. Society

TITLES IN THIS SERIES

WOMEN'S RIGHTS
ON THE FRONTIER

THERESE DeANGELIS

MASON CREST
PHILADELPHIA

J 323.3 D

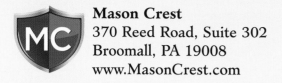

Mason Crest
370 Reed Road, Suite 302
Broomall, PA 19008
www.MasonCrest.com

CPSIA Compliance Information: Batch #FF2012-4. For further information, contact Mason Crest at 1-866-MCP-Book.

First printing
1 3 5 7 9 8 6 4 2

Library of Congress Cataloging-in-Publication Data

DeAngelis, Therese.
  Women's rights on the frontier / Therese DeAngelis.
      p. cm. — (Finding a voice : women's fight for equality in U.S. society)
  Includes bibliographical references and index.
  ISBN 978-1-4222-2359-8 (hc)
  ISBN 978-1-4222-2369-7 (pb)
  1. Women's right—United States—History—Juvenile literature. 2. Women—
Suffrage—United States—Juvenile literature. 3. Women—Suffrage—West (U.S.)—
Juvenile literature. I. Title.
  HQ1236.5.U6D43 2012
  323.3'40973—dc23

                                        2011043485

Publisher's note: All quotations in this book are taken from original sources, and contain the spelling and grammatical inconsistencies of the original texts.

Picture credits: Kansas Historical Society: 27; Library of Congress: 11, 12, 13, 14, 19, 20 (top), 30, 34, 35, 36, 37, 39, 40, 41, 43, 44, 46, 48, 49, 51, 52, 55; National Archives: 15, 20 (bottom), 31, 37; © 2011 Photos.com, a division of Getty Images: 17, 21, 22, 23; Wikimedia Commons: 29; Women's Rights National Historical Park: 8.

TABLE OF CONTENTS

INTRODUCTION

As the Executive Director of the Sewall-Belmont House & Museum, which is the fifth and final headquarters of the historic National Woman's Party (NWP), I am surrounded each day by artifacts that give voice to the stories of Alice Paul, Lucy Burns, Doris Stevens, Alva Belmont, and the whole community of women who waged an intense campaign for the right to vote during the second decade of the 20th century. The

A. Page Harrington, director, Sewall-Belmont House & Museum

original photographs, documents, protest banners, and magnificent floor-length capes worn by these courageous activists during marches and demonstrations help us bring their work to life for the many groups who tour the museum each week.

The perseverance of the suffragists bore fruit in 1920, with the ratification of the 19th Amendment. It was a huge milestone, though certainly not the end of the journey toward full equality for American women.

Throughout much (if not most) of American history, social conventions and the law constrained female participation in the political, economic, and intellectual life of the nation. Women's voices were routinely stifled, their contributions downplayed or dismissed, their potential ignored. Underpinning this state of affairs was a widely held assumption of male superiority in most spheres of human endeavor.

Always, however, there were women who gave the lie to gender-based stereotypes. Some helped set the national agenda. For example, in the years preceding the Revolutionary War, Mercy Otis Warren made a compelling case for American independence through her writings. Abigail Adams, every bit the intellectual equal of her husband, counseled John Adams to "remember the ladies and be more generous and favorable to them than your ancestors" when creating laws for the new country. Sojourner Truth helped lead the movement to abolish slavery in the 19th century. A hundred years later, Rosa Parks galvanized the civil rights movement, which finally secured for African Americans the promise of equality under the law.

The lives of these women are familiar today. So, too, are the stories of groundbreakers such as astronaut Sally Ride; Supreme Court justice Sandra Day O'Connor; and Nancy Pelosi, Speaker of the House of Representatives.

But famous figures are only part of the story. The path toward gender equality was also paved—and American society shaped—by countless women whose individual lives and deeds have never been chronicled in depth. These include the women who toiled alongside their fathers and brothers and husbands on the western frontier; the women who kept U.S. factories running during World War II; and the women who worked tirelessly to promote the goals of the modern feminist movement.

The FINDING A VOICE series tells the stories of famous and anonymous women alike. Together these volumes provide a wide-ranging overview of American women's long quest to achieve full equality with men—a quest that continues today.

The Sewall-Belmont House & Museum is located at 144 Constitution Avenue in Washington, D.C. You can find out more on the Web at www.sewallbelmont.org

In July 1848, five women—Jane Hunt, Mary Ann M'Clintock, Lucretia Mott, Martha C. Wright, and Elizabeth Cady Stanton—met at the M'Clintock home in Waterloo, New York. There, the women drafted a document that they called the "Declaration of Sentiments," which called for equal social and political rights for American women. This declaration would create a sensation several days later, when it was publicly presented during the first Woman's Rights Convention in nearby Seneca Falls.

1

THE LONG PATH TO EQUALITY

Charlotte Woodward Pierce remembered the summer day in 1848 when she first heard about a meeting for women's rights. She was 19 years old and living in Waterloo, New York. Charlotte lived with Moses Chapman and his wife, Hannah, who were farmers. Charlotte worked at home, sewing gloves made from pieces of leather sent to her by merchants. But she was not paid for her work. Instead, her wages went to Moses Chapman.

Charlotte hated being a glove maker. She did not mind working hard, but she believed she should earn money for her labor. She also wanted to choose her own job, instead of being forced to do work that others decided was suitable for a young woman.

A QUESTION OF CHOICE

During the 19th century, women did not have the same rights as men. Few women had the chance to attend college. For those who did go to school, not many jobs were available. Most women quit working after they married, so that they could raise children and run the household. But if a married woman continued to work, her pay belonged to her husband.

In nearly every state, a married woman could not legally own property. Even if parents or relatives had named her the owner of the property, by law it belonged to her husband once she married. If a woman's husband abused her, she could not divorce him or gain custody of her children. Women were not allowed to vote for representatives in their state's governing body, or legislature. They could not hold elected office. Before 1850, women in America were not even counted in the population census.

Charlotte's friends seemed as unhappy as she was. "I do not believe there was any community anywhere in which the souls of some women were not beating their wings in rebellion," she told an interviewer many years later. "I wanted to work, but I wanted to choose my task and I wanted to collect my wages."

GOING TO SENECA FALLS

The convention was scheduled for July 19 and 20 at the Wesleyan Methodist Church in Seneca Falls, about 40 miles from Waterloo. Charlotte was so excited that she immediately ran to her friends' homes to tell them about it. Many had already heard the news. Some were very interested and wanted to attend.

Attending the Seneca Falls Convention would take great courage. In the 1840s, respectable women did not speak in public. Women avoided draw-

FAST FACT

Why weren't married women's rights recognized in early America? Because the men who wrote the U.S. Constitution and the state constitutions adapted English common law for their purposes. Under English law, when a women married she became "one unity with the husband." In other words, she legally ceased to exist as an independent person. All her property went to her husband, and he voted on her behalf.

ELIZABETH CADY STANTON (1815–1902)

Elizabeth Cady Stanton learned early that women were not treated equally: After her father lost his last surviving son, he told his 11-year-old daughter that he wished she had been a boy. She decided at that moment that she would strive to be equal to men in all things. The leader of the Seneca Falls Convention believed that women would not achieve equality unless they claimed their right to vote. In partnership with Susan B. Anthony, she wrote and argued fiercely for women's equality through suffrage.

ing attention to themselves. Charlotte and her friends worried about what would happen if they attended. In the end, however, they decided to go.

Early on July 19, the young women climbed into a horse-drawn wagon for the long journey. As they neared Seneca Falls, they noticed many other wagons and carriages headed for the same destination. Nearly all of the passengers were women.

FROM FEAR TO COURAGE

The first day of the convention was advertised for women only. But when Charlotte and her friends arrived at the church, they saw many men also waiting to enter. Charlotte had planned to attend only the first day's meeting and then return home. When she saw that so many men supported equal rights for women, she was encouraged to stay for both days.

The Seneca Falls Convention made history. It was the first women's rights convention ever held in the United States. In addition to the 40 men that Charlotte saw, more than 300 women attended.

Five women had organized the meeting: Elizabeth Cady Stanton, Lucretia Mott, Martha Coffin Wright, Jane Hunt, and Mary Ann

M'Clintock. They drew up a document based on the Declaration of Independence. In this Declaration of Sentiments and Resolutions, they demanded equal civil rights for women. This included property ownership, legal issues, and wage earning.

Sixty-eight women and 32 men signed the declaration. The only resolution on which every signer did not agree was the call for suffrage—the right to vote.

HOW IMPORTANT IS THE RIGHT TO VOTE?

This may seem surprising today. At the time, however, most women's rights advocates thought that securing other rights was more urgent. For example, they believed women should be able to own property legally. They wanted the right to attend college. They demanded to be able to secure jobs of their own choosing and keep the wages they earned. They wanted fair divorce laws, so that a woman could keep her children if her marriage should fail.

LUCRETIA MOTT (1793–1880)

Lucretia Mott was a Quaker and an abolitionist when she met Elizabeth Cady Stanton. Unlike Stanton, Mott says that she "grew up so thoroughly imbued with women's rights that it was the most important question of my life from a very early day." She believed women should train themselves to take their rightful places in society beside men. After the Thirteenth Amendment abolished slavery, most other abolitionists believed their work was done. But Lucretia Mott remained dedicated throughout her life to securing full civil rights both for African Americans and women.

ANOTHER VOICE FOR EQUAL RIGHTS

Frederick Douglass, a former slave and a powerful abolitionist, spoke at the Seneca Falls Convention. He was among the men who signed the Declaration of Sentiments. Douglass compared women's battle for suffrage with the struggle to abolish slavery. "Many who have at last made the discovery that the negroes have some rights . . . have yet to be convinced that women are entitled to any," he wrote in the July 28, 1848, issue of his newspaper, *The North Star*. "We hold woman to be justly entitled to all [rights] we claim for man. . . . All that distinguishes man as an intelligent and accountable being, is equally true of woman."

Elizabeth Cady Stanton later credited Douglass with persuading the signers of the Declaration to pass the ninth resolution, which demanded suffrage.

The idea that women's right to vote would be legally recognized seemed like a far-off dream. The conference leaders feared that if they demanded suffrage too soon, leaders and lawmakers would not take them seriously. They did not want to risk losing ground on the other rights they fought for.

"MY HEART IS WITH ALL THE WOMEN WHO VOTE"

The Nineteenth Amendment to the U.S. Constitution, which guarantees all American women their right to vote, did not pass until 1920—seventy-two years after the Seneca Falls Convention. By that time, only one woman who had participated in the convention was still alive: Charlotte Woodward Pierce.

Charlotte probably never had the opportunity to vote, however. On Election Day in 1920, she was 91 years old and too ill to leave her home.

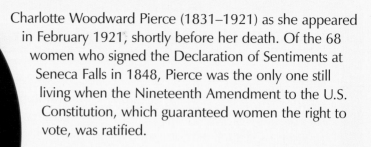

Charlotte Woodward Pierce (1831–1921) as she appeared in February 1921, shortly before her death. Of the 68 women who signed the Declaration of Sentiments at Seneca Falls in 1848, Pierce was the only one still living when the Nineteenth Amendment to the U.S. Constitution, which guaranteed women the right to vote, was ratified.

"I'm afraid I'll never vote," she said, noting her advanced age. But she remained a strong supporter of women's suffrage until her death. "My heart is with all women who vote," she said. "They have gained it now, and they should not quarrel about the method of using it."

Throughout the 72 years from 1848 to 1920, supporters of women's suffrage worked hard to advance their cause. They fought unjust laws. They held conventions and parades to make more people aware of the issue. They formed their own organizations to lobby for new laws. They presented lectures to encourage discussion of women's suffrage.

At times these women were mocked and humiliated. Many were jailed and even physically abused after protesting outside the White House. Nevertheless, they continued their struggle with courage and perseverance.

BRINGING THE BATTLE WESTWARD

During the 1840s, women were also helping to shape the United States as it expanded westward. Side by side with men, they settled in U.S. territories, where they helped to clear land and build homes and towns. They married, set up households, and raised families in parts of the country that previously had been wilderness.

Not many Americans lived in the frontier territories. To establish their homesteads, women on the frontier often had to help their husbands with work that women living in the established U.S. states would never have

WOMEN AT WORK

After the American Revolution ended in 1783, the new country required more workers to establish and maintain settlements. Women were in demand as laborers outside the home. Those who lived in frontier communities performed physically taxing work as they established households and farmed land.

As women's roles grew more varied, the social and legal restrictions regarding their rights gradually changed. In 1787, for example, the Massachusetts legislature allowed women who were abandoned by their husbands to sell property. Women also gained the right to be elected to public office. Few women held such positions. One exception was Mary Katherine Goddard, a newspaper publisher who served as postmaster of Baltimore from 1775 to 1789.

By the end of the 18th century, the ways in which women lived and worked in American society had begun to shift. Over the next few decades, women would increasingly demand legal and economic reforms. These reforms would bring them closer to achieving equal rights with men.

been expected to do. For this reason, women's rights supporters realized that the territories might be the best places to gain a foothold for women's suffrage.

They were right. In the Western territories of Wyoming, Utah, Colorado, and Washington, women were legally permitted to vote many years before the federal government acknowledged that right. Suffrage victories in the West helped pave the way for the passage of the Nineteenth Amendment. How this happened is a remarkable story of determined women who refused to settle for less than full citizenship.

WOMEN'S RIGHT TO VOTE

The U.S. Constitution never specifically prohibited women from voting. Women legally voted in some states at the time the Declaration of Independence was drafted in 1776. In Massachusetts, New Hampshire, New Jersey, and New York, unmarried women who owned property could cast ballots in elections. But the state constitutions were soon rewritten. Women in New York lost the right to vote in 1777. In 1780, the Massachusetts State Constitution specified "male" as a qualification. In 1784, women's right to vote was taken away in New Hampshire. And in 1807, New Jersey rescinded women's suffrage. It was not until the Nineteenth Amendment to the U.S. Constitution was ratified in 1920 that the right of American women to vote was guaranteed.

2

A GROWING DISCONTENT

At the end of the 18th century, women in the United States, England, and elsewhere began to speak out publicly against legal and social restrictions placed on them. One of the most outspoken was Mary Wollstonecraft.

Wollstonecraft, a resident of Great Britain, had published a book called *Vindication of the Rights of Woman* in 1792. She argued that limiting women's right to an education kept them in a state of "ignorance, and slavish dependence." She criticized societies in which women were expected to be passive and more concerned with their appearance than with important social issues.

Wollstonecraft thought that for women, marriage amounted to slavery. She warned that treating women this way not only harmed women; it also harmed all of society. Women "may be convenient slaves," she wrote, "but slavery will have its constant effect, degrading the master and the abject dependent."

Wollstonecraft's book caused enormous controversy. She was mocked, criticized, and called names. Still, she continued to argue that women should have the same opportunities and rights claimed by

Mary Wollstonecraft

men. Her views were vastly different from those of most men—and many women—of the time.

"THE ORDER OF NATURE"

A few women agreed with Wollstonecraft's views on women's civil rights. In 1818, a Boston essay writer named Hannah Crocker published *Observations on the Real Rights of Women*. She too argued that education was the key to helping women achieve equal rights.

Before she married in 1779, Crocker had opened a school for women. Her aim was to prove that they had the same capacity for intelligence as men—if they were given the same educational opportunities to develop it.

Crocker disagreed with Wollstonecraft on important points, however. She thought that women were not meant to engage in the same occupations as men, even though they were smart enough. Among their "rights," she concluded, were the rights to be virtuous, loving, religious, and sympathetic to men.

Women, Crocker argued, were meant to train the next generation and to teach peace and virtue. "For the interest of their country, or in the cause of humanity," she wrote, "we shall strictly adhere to the principle and the impropriety of females ever trespassing on masculine grounds, as it is morally incorrect, and physically improper."

"THINKING BEINGS"

In 1818, 23-year-old Frances "Fanny" Wright traveled to the United States to see the new country firsthand. She had educated herself in the library of Glasgow College in Scotland, where she became fascinated with the history of America and its principles of independence.

During her two years in the United States, Wright wrote *Views of Society and Manners in America*. She praised the new American government as being progressive and open to new ideas. "The women are assuming their place as thinking beings, not in despite of the men, but chiefly in consequence of [men's] enlarged views and exertions as fathers and legislators," she wrote.

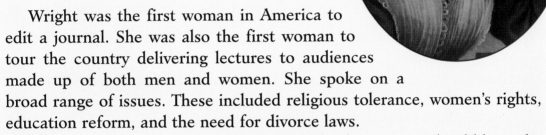

British-born activist Frances "Fanny" Wright (1795–1852) was an outspoken critic of slavery and a supporter of woman's rights. During her 1828–29 lecture tour of the United States, she caused a national sensation by speaking to audiences composed of both men and women.

Wright was the first woman in America to edit a journal. She was also the first woman to tour the country delivering lectures to audiences made up of both men and women. She spoke on a broad range of issues. These included religious tolerance, women's rights, education reform, and the need for divorce laws.

Like Mary Wollstonecraft, Wright thought that women should have the right to acquire as much formal education as they desired. She also believed that women should play a larger role in society than keeping a household and raising children. Just like Mary Wollstonecraft, however, Wright was scorned and ridiculed by those who didn't agree. She required a bodyguard while traveling. Protesters at her public appearances sometimes became violent.

A TURNING POINT

Fanny Wright died four years after the Seneca Falls Convention. In later years, her views on America had changed somewhat. She no longer felt as positive about the United States as when she had first arrived more than 30 years earlier.

By this time, however, American women had reason to feel hopeful. A move to reform all areas of American society had begun in the 1830s. The two most active groups were the abolitionists and the temperance movement, which was against the use of alcoholic beverages. Women joined both movements in great force.

"A MORAL THERMOMETER"

In 1790, Philadelphia physician Benjamin Rush published an anti-alcohol book detailing the horrors of drunkenness. The book included a diagram of a "moral thermometer." Those who abstained from alcohol appeared at the top. They had "Health, Wealth, Serenity of mind, Reputation, long life, and Happiness." Those who consumed alcohol appeared at the base of the thermometer. They were described with lists of "Vices, Diseases, and Punishments," ending in "Suicide, Death, or Gallows [hanging]." Rush's book was hugely popular, and by the 1830s a national temperance movement was underway. Temperance was taught in schools, and legislators passed laws in support of the cause.

Frances Willard

Members of temperance groups came from all classes, religions, and races. Many were also involved in anti-slavery and women's suffrage activities. The Woman's Christian Temperance Union (WCTU), founded in 1874 in Cleveland, Ohio, gained 25,000 members within a few years. Under the leadership of Frances Willard, the WCTU gave important support to the women's suffrage movement. By 1883, it had spread worldwide and was renamed the World's Woman's Christian Temperance Union.

Saloons like these were common in frontier towns during the late 19th century.

In 1848, the year of the Seneca Falls Convention, several major events helped to change how women perceived their roles in American society.

SEEKING GOLD

In January 1848, gold was discovered in the mountains of California. Over the next two years, "gold fever" swept the globe. More than 300,000 people traveled to California from around the world with the hope of becoming instantly wealthy.

Families who were already in California farming were among the first to arrive in the gold-mining fields. Men brought their wives and children. All of them worked side by side. Among the thousands of later arrivals who traveled overland—called "Forty-Niners" because they arrived in 1849—about 10 percent were women. With so many people flocking to the gold-mining area, towns and settlements sprang up almost overnight. California's population in 1850 was almost 100,000; just ten years later, it was 380,000.

Women of all races and classes participated in the gold rush. Some came with husbands and families. Others came on their own, seeking adventure or a new way of life. These women sought wealth, but they also

When gold was discovered in the California territory in 1848, many women traveled west with their husbands hoping to strike it rich. Although relatively few became wealthy through mining, life in the gold fields offered a chance for women to take on nontraditional work.

A wagon train travels westward across the American prairie, circa 1870. Beginning in the 1840s, thousands of pioneer families traveled west, looking to establish homes in sparsely settled frontier territories.

sought business and social opportunities not available in the eastern states.

The journey from the established East Coast states to an untamed area on the other side of the continent was very dangerous. Many of those who set out for the West Coast did not survive the trip. Disease, accidents, and other misfortunes were common on the long and difficult trek across the country. Nor was life easy for those who arrived safely. Still, for the women who successfully reached California, pioneer life was filled with opportunity.

EXPANSION, SLAVERY, AND WOMEN'S RIGHTS

Just a few weeks after the gold discovery, the United States signed the Treaty of Guadalupe-Hidalgo, ending a two-year war with Mexico. Under the terms of the treaty, Mexico ceded almost half of its territory to the United States in exchange for $15 million. This was a huge expanse of land. The territory included modern-day California, Arizona, New Mexico, and Texas, and parts of Colorado, Nevada, and Utah.

One result of this expansion was a renewed debate over slavery. The leaders of states in the South, where slavery was permitted, wanted to see slavery allowed in California and the other new territories. Most leaders of the Northern states, where slavery was illegal, did not want slavery to expand into the western territories. Abolitionists, of course, wanted to outlaw slavery throughout the United States.

Many women who wanted to secure women's rights were also active abolitionists. Unfortunately, this did not mean that they were always treated equally by abolitionist groups. For example, the American Anti-Slavery Society, which had been founded in 1833 in Philadelphia, accepted women as members, but it did not allow them to speak at gatherings. Speaking in public was thought coarse and unwomanly.

African-American slaves pick cotton on a southern plantation. The issue of slavery—essential to the South's agricultural economy, but outlawed in the North—bitterly divided the nation during the mid-1800s. Women were an important element of the abolitionist movement, which sought to eliminate slavery in the United States.

THE BIRTH OF
THE WOMEN'S RIGHTS MOVEMENT

Before long, however, so many women had joined the abolitionist movement that they were free to form their own anti-slavery societies and speak as they wished. Elizabeth Cady Stanton offered her first public speech in 1841 in Seneca Falls. She spoke to 100 women on the subject of temperance, but she also introduced another issue. As she later wrote a friend, "I infused into my speech [a] . . . dose of woman's rights, as I take good care to do in many private conversations."

The Seneca Falls Convention of 1848 sparked a series of state and local conventions. On October 23 and 24, 1850, Lucy Stone and other Seneca Falls organizers held the first National Woman's Rights Convention in Worcester, Massachusetts. About 1,000 people attended. Members resolved to support "equality before the law, without distinction of sex or color."

In 1870, Elizabeth Cady Stanton wrote that the movement to secure women's rights "may be dated from the first National Convention, held at Worcester, Mass., October, 1850." For Stanton—and for many other women—the 1850 convention marked the birth of the first organized women's rights movement. It's notable that the women who participated also formally recognized that African Americans and others also required equal rights.

3

THE BATTLE FOR SUFFRAGE

As the United States expanded, women's rights supporters traveled westward. They sought areas where female pioneers had helped settle the country. In those regions, they reasoned, inhabitants and lawmakers would be more open to granting women the right to vote. After all, women had already proved that they could contribute as much to pioneer society as men had.

Women's rights supporters had another reason for traveling to western frontier areas. Laws and social customs there tended to be less limiting to women. The western territories and the newest states had fewer social restrictions than eastern states. In addition, the kind of laws that were common in older states—such as those that prevented married women from owning property—had not taken a firm hold on the frontier.

THE PUSH FOR NEW LAWS

One of the greatest goals of the women's suffrage movement was to lobby for new laws that favored equality for women. Clarina Nichols, who left Vermont in 1854 to travel to Kansas and help secure voting rights, explained why the strategy was important. "It was a thousand times more difficult to procure the repeal of unjust laws in an old State, than the adoption of just laws in the organization of a new State," she wrote.

To accomplish this task, members of women's suffrage organizations traveled throughout the new territories to speak about women's rights.

They wanted as many Americans as possible to hear and think about broader rights for women. They delivered public lectures on the subject. They also met with lawmakers to convince them to discuss women's suffrage in territorial legislatures and in constitutional conventions.

The strategy was successful in some cases. As early as 1846, delegates to the Wisconsin constitutional convention adopted a law allowing married women to own property. The law was later dropped after voters rejected the constitution. In 1853, however, shortly after Wisconsin became a state, the property law was restored.

THE MEANING OF "UNIVERSAL"

Women's suffrage supporters faced overwhelming obstacles trying to persuade lawmakers to broaden voting rights. At times, even a small issue—for example, the wording of a legal provision—could mean the difference in gaining the chance for suffrage.

When Indiana lawmakers gathered to revise the state constitution in 1850, a delegate named Nathan B. Hawkins suggested a provision for "universal suffrage." The provision suggested that current voters decide the issue in a general election. (At the time, Indiana permitted only free white male citizens older than 21 years to vote.)

The phrase "universal suffrage" commonly describes voting rights for all Americans. But another delegate, Daniel Kelso, questioned Hawkins' meaning. "According to our general understanding of the right to universal suffrage, I have no objection to the adoption of the resolution," he said. "But if it be the intention . . . to extend the right of suffrage to females and negroes, I am against it." To Kelso, "universal" had an entirely different meaning. "I understand this language to be the measure of universal suffrage: that there shall be no property qualifications, no religious tests," he explained. In his view, the state already allowed voting rights for all who were eligible. He did not consider women and non-white Americans worthy of suffrage.

SLOW BUT STEADY

The idea of women's suffrage gradually gained ground in frontier regions. Even when laws granting rights to women did not pass, they made people think about and discuss the issues.

In 1859, Clarina Nichols presented petitions to a Kansas constitutional convention demanding that women's voting rights be recognized. The delegates listened to her argument and debated the matter, but they rejected the provision. They feared that including women's suffrage in the territorial constitution would hurt their chance of achieving statehood.

Nichols was not completely unsuccessful, however. She convinced the delegates to give women the right to vote in school district elections. The Kansas constitution also included provisions that would protect the right of women to own property and care for their children.

At an 1859 convention held to write a new constitution for the Kansas territory, some delegates supported granting equal voting rights to Kansas women. The majority, however, would not accept this "radical" idea, and suffrage was granted only to white men age 21 and older. The Wyandotte Constitution—named for the town where the constitutional convention was held—did give Kansas women certain rights that were not guaranteed elsewhere in the United States at that time. The Wyandotte Constitution was ratified in October 1859, and went into effect when Kansas was admitted as a U.S. State in January 1861.

CIVIL WAR

When the Civil War broke out in 1861, most suffragists ceased campaigning for women's rights. They believed they could serve their country better by devoting themselves to the war effort.

While men were at war, American women "managed the farm, the shop, the office, as well as the family," according to one Wisconsin woman. Some participated more directly. Clara Barton and Dorothea Dix organized a national nursing corps for wounded and ill soldiers. Elizabeth Cady Stanton and Susan B. Anthony helped convince Congress to pass the Thirteenth Amendment, which would abolish slavery (the amendment became law in December 1865). Thousands of women volunteered with the U.S. Sanitary Commission to support Union soldiers.

A RENEWED EFFORT

After the Civil War ended in 1865, women returned to the work of claiming voting rights. Many had gained new experience in occupations that previously had been denied to women. They had also learned the value of organizing to achieve their goals. With new enthusiasm, they set off once more to western territories and states.

THE U.S. SANITARY COMMISSION

In 1861, the federal government established the U.S. Sanitary Commission to coordinate women's volunteer war efforts. Under the commission, women raised $25 million for the Union army. They worked as nurses, sewed uniforms, operated Army camp kitchens, and arranged lodging for soldiers who were traveling or disabled. In 1864, President Abraham Lincoln paid them tribute: "If all that has been said by orators and poets . . . in praise of women, were applied to the women of America, it would not do them justice. . . . God bless the women of America!"

SERVING HER COUNTRY

Although women were forbidden to enlist in the military during the Civil War, more than 200 of them disguised themselves as men and joined the fight. One of the most famous was Sarah Emma Edmonds (pictured). She joined the Union's Second Michigan Infantry as Franklin Thompson. During the war, Edmonds served as a male field nurse, a mail orderly, and a brigade postmaster. While on special assignments for the Secret Service, she broke through Confederate lines "disguised" as a woman. Edmonds received a military pension in 1886.

Although slavery had been abolished with passage of the Thirteenth Amendment, the U.S. government had not yet recognized African Americans' right to vote. After the war, women who had fought for abolition and for women's voting rights now joined groups fighting to gain African-American suffrage.

In 1866, Elizabeth Cady Stanton, Susan B. Anthony, and other women joined with African-American activists like Frederick Douglass. They formed a new organization called the American Equal Rights Association (AERA). The group's members wanted to combine the efforts of those who supported voting rights for women and African Americans. The AERA's aim, they said, was to "secure Equal Rights to all American citizens, especially the right of suffrage, irrespective of race, color, or sex."

EARLY DEFEAT

The first test of whether the AERA would be effective came in 1867. In Kansas, the state legislature approved one referendum on women's suffrage and another on black suffrage. With women's rights groups, the

AERA waged a strong campaign to see that both amendments passed. Along with Stanton and Anthony, other women's rights leaders such as Lucy Stone traveled to Kansas to fight for the measures.

To their great disappointment, both amendments were defeated. The political loss was the first of many that women's rights supporters would suffer over the next 40 years. Beginning in 1870, 11 states, nearly all of which were western, held 17 referenda for women's voting rights. But by 1910, only four states had recognized full suffrage for women.

A RIFT IN THE WOMEN'S RIGHTS MOVEMENT

In February 1869, Congress proposed an amendment to the U.S. Constitution that would make it illegal to deny a citizen the right to vote based on "race, color, or previous condition of servitude [slavery]." This meant that if the amendment passed, former male African-American slaves could claim their right to vote.

Women were not named in the amendment. Those who had supported the AERA were angry and upset. They believed the Fifteenth Amendment should also give women the right to vote. Some women, such as Susan B.

LUCY STONE (1818–1893)

Lucy Stone helped organize the 1850 National Woman's Rights Convention, held in Worcester, Massachusetts. When she married fellow abolitionist Henry B. Blackwell in 1855, the couple read and signed a document protesting a husband's legal rights over his wife. In 1870, she cofounded the *Woman's Journal*, a weekly suffrage publication. She edited the journal until 1882 when her daughter, Alice Stone Blackwell, took over.

Fortieth Congress of the United States of America;

At the *third* Session,

Begun and held at the city of Washington, on Monday, the *seventh* day of *December*, one thousand eight hundred and *sixty-eight*.

A RESOLUTION

Proposing an amendment to the Constitution of the United States.

Resolved by the Senate and House of Representatives of the United States of America in Congress assembled, (two-thirds of both Houses concurring) That the following article be proposed to the legislatures of the several States as an amendment to the Constitution of the United States, which, when ratified by three-fourths of said legislatures shall be valid as part of the Constitution, namely:

Article XV.

Section 1. The right of citizens of the United States to vote shall not be denied or abridged by the United States or by any State on account of race, color, or previous condition of servitude.—

Section 2. The Congress shall have power to enforce this article by appropriate legislation.—

Schuyler Colfax
Speaker of the House of Representatives.

B. F. Wade
President of the Senate pro tempore.

Attest:
Edw. McPherson
Clerk of House of Representatives.

Although women had been instrumental in achieving passage and ratification of the Fifteenth Amendment to the U.S. Constitution in 1870, the amendment failed to address the issue of women's voting rights.

Anthony and Elizabeth Cady Stanton, felt that other AERA leaders had betrayed them by negotiating African-American suffrage without demanding women's suffrage. They asked the AERA to support another amendment giving women the right to vote. When they were turned down, the two women abandoned the association.

Anthony and Stanton quickly formed their own all-female organization, the National Woman Suffrage Association (NWSA). That same year, more conservative women's rights leaders established another group, the American Woman Suffrage Association (AWSA). The organizers of this group included Lucy Stone and Julia Ward Howe.

The division between the NWSA and AWSA was based on beliefs about African-American civil rights and how they were related to women's civil rights. Members of NWSA would not support a constitutional amendment that left out women's suffrage—even if it recognized suffrage for blacks. AWSA members, on the other hand, were willing to support expanded civil rights for blacks immediately—even if it meant that they would not yet gain voting rights themselves.

The Fifteenth Amendment was ratified on February 3, 1870. But the rift between NWSA and AWSA members would continue for two decades.

4

WESTERN MILESTONES

The women's movement suffered some disappointing losses in the West, but it also enjoyed landmark successes. Although the Kansas effort of 1867 was unsuccessful, it marked the first referendum on women's suffrage ever held in the United States. Two years later, on December 10, 1869, Wyoming Territory passed the first full women's suffrage law in the United States.

PLANNING AHEAD

One reason the law succeeded in Wyoming Territory was that those who were opposed to women's suffrage did not have time to organize a campaign. Those who proposed the law, however, had carefully planned their arguments.

Territorial Secretary Edward M. Lee and legislator William H. Bright introduced the bill to the Wyoming legislature. Both men recognized the important role women had played in establishing frontier settlements. Bright's wife, Julia, was a women's rights advocate. So was Esther Morris, a friend of the Brights. Lee himself had long supported women's suffrage. He argued that it was unfair that his mother did not have the right to vote when African Americans already did.

Map of U.S. territories and states between the Mississippi River and the Pacific Coast, 1867. Through a series of wars and transactions during the first half of the 19th century, the United States gained control over a vast tract of western land. These acquired territories would eventually be admitted as states; before that could occur, however, each territory had to be settled and to establish a constitutional government that was in alignment with the U.S. system. Unlike in the established states, however, residents of the territories had some latitude in the rights that could be provided for citizens under their local constitutions—including the right for women to vote, own property, and hold public office.

Bright and Lee also argued that passing the law would benefit the territory. Wyoming was rugged and remote, with a population of more than 6,000 men and only 1,000 women. If the law passed, women might find Wyoming a more attractive place to live. It would provide good "advertising" for Wyoming Territory and would draw women and families to the region.

Other legislators may have had less noble reasons for supporting the bill. All 20 members of the Wyoming legislature were Democrats. Some people believed that many legislators supported the bill because they wanted to embarrass the Republican governor, John A. Campbell. If the legislature passed the bill, it would next go to Campbell for approval. Most politicians assumed that the governor would veto the bill. If he did, they could blame the bill's failure on the governor and take credit for having supported women's right to vote.

ESTHER HOBART MORRIS (1814–1902)

Esther Hobart Morris was born in New York state. Orphaned at 11, she was apprenticed to a seamstress and eventually became a successful milliner and businesswoman. After her husband died in 1845, Esther moved to Peru, Illinois, to settle her husband's estate. The difficulties she encountered made her realize the legal complexities faced by women. In 1869 she moved with her second husband, John Morris, to a gold rush camp in Wyoming Territory. To promote the idea of recognizing women's right to vote, she organized a tea party for the electors and candidates of the first territorial legislature. She became the first woman ever to serve as justice of the peace when she was appointed for the South Pass District in 1870. Morris was recognized as a suffrage pioneer during Wyoming's 1890 statehood celebration. Five years later, at 80 years old, she became a delegate to the national suffrage convention in Cleveland, Ohio.

THE EQUALITY STATE

Governor Campbell did not act as some legislators expected. He knew that if he signed the bill into law, Wyoming would gain national attention as the first territory or state ever to confirm women's right to vote. He signed the bill.

Esther Morris later told a newspaper reporter, "the whole matter of the adoption of Woman Suffrage in the Territory was the result of a bitter feud between the existing political parties." She believed "it was done in a moment of spite—not out of any regard for the movement." Nonetheless, women in the Wyoming Territory now possessed a fundamental right of citizenship that no other U.S. women had yet attained.

The new Wyoming law did not just give women the right to vote. It also allowed women to hold political office and serve on juries. The year after the law passed, Esther Morris and Caroline Neil became America's first female justices of the peace. In March 1870, the first jury in the country to include women convened in Laramie. In September 1870, Eliza A. Swain became the first woman in Wyoming to cast a legal ballot in an election.

In 1871, women's rights advocates Elizabeth Cady Stanton (seated) and Susan B. Anthony toured the Western territories. They spoke to large audiences in Wyoming, Utah, and elsewhere, including a speech before 5,000 women at the Mormon Tabernacle in Salt Lake City on June 27, 1871.

"LAND OF FREEDOM"

Those who believed that the suffrage law would draw people to Wyoming were correct. Word quickly spread across the country. Tourists and journalists traveled westward to see its effects. What they saw were ordinary women, living their lives as usual. In towns, Wyoming women helped organize schools and churches. Ranch women raised cattle and hunted game. A few African-American women found employment in larger towns such as Cheyenne.

Susan B. Anthony was so delighted by news of the law's passage that she urged East Coast women to migrate immediately to Wyoming. No great migration of women occurred. However, in 1871, Anthony and Elizabeth Cady Stanton traveled together to what they called the "land of freedom" on the newly completed Transcontinental Railroad.

When they arrived in Laramie, one hundred admiring women greeted their train. "We have been moving over the soil that is really the land of the free and the home of the brave . . . in which women are the recognized political equals of men," Anthony later wrote. "Women here can say: 'What a magnificent country is ours, where every class and caste, color and sex, may find equal freedom.'"

When Wyoming Territory's leaders prepared for statehood in 1889, they included

Wyoming was not only the first U.S. territory to recognize women's right to vote and the first to allow women to serve on juries. In 1924, it also became the first state to elect a woman governor, Nellie Tayloe Ross (1876–1977). Ross was later appointed the first female director of the U.S. Mint, a position she held for 20 years.

WOMAN SUFFRAGE IN WYOMING TERRITORY.—SCENE AT THE POLLS IN CHEYENNE.
FROM A PHOTO. BY KIRKLAND.—SEE PAGE 747.

This illustration from the November 24, 1888, issue of *Frank Leslie's Illustrated Newspaper* depicts women voting in Cheyenne, Wyoming. When this article appeared, the territory was preparing to apply for statehood, and the idea of a state where women could vote seemed unusual to many Americans.

a provision for women's suffrage in their constitution. In 1890, Wyoming became the first state to enter the Union with full suffrage for women.

RELIGIOUS RIGHTS AND WOMEN'S SUFFRAGE

In 1870, Utah Territory also recognized full voting rights for women. But the story of how this came about is very different from that of Wyoming.

Single men made up the greatest part of the population in nearly all western territories and states. Utah Territory, however, was settled by Mormons who had fled religious persecution. The Mormons practiced polygamy, which means that men were allowed to be married to more than one woman at a time. Instead of single men, Utah's population was mostly made up of families—including a large proportion of women. When the territory approved the law permitting women's suffrage, more than 17,000 women became eligible to vote. At the time, this was the largest population of female voters in the world.

One of the most outspoken leaders for women's rights, Emmeline B. Wells, was a strong supporter of polygamy. Although most people believed that women's rights and polygamy were contradictory ideas, Wells did not agree. She believed that every woman had a right to determine her own destiny.

Two Mormon women stand outside their homestead with their children, circa 1887.

Wells argued that a "plural marriage" gave a woman personal freedom to exercise her rights as a member of society. If a woman was capable of exercising her right to vote for lawmakers, Wells said, then she was also capable of choosing whom she would marry. "I believe in women, especially thinking women," she wrote.

FROM WASHINGTON, D.C., TO UTAH TERRITORY

The question of women's suffrage in Utah first arose in 1868 in Washington, D.C. George W. Julian, an Indiana congressman, introduced

A longtime supporter of expanded rights for women, George Washington Julian (1817–1899) represented Indiana in the U.S. Congress. His proposed 1868 legislation would have given women the right to vote in the District of Columbia as well as in the western territories.

a bill in the U.S. House of Representatives that would legalize women's suffrage in all the western territories. Congressman Hamilton Wilcox of New York, another supporter, agreed with Julian.

Recognizing the voting rights of women in the territories, Wilcox said, would help persuade more women to settle there. He also believed that if Utah women exercised their right to vote, they would almost certainly vote to abolish polygamy—which many non-Mormons, suffragists, and members of U.S. Congress found distasteful.

Julian's bill failed. However, the delegate from Utah Territory, William H. Hooper, liked the idea. He and other Mormon leaders thought that recognizing women's right to vote in Utah would benefit the territory and would not lead to the abolishment of polygamy.

Newspaper articles supported the idea. "Our ladies can prove to the world that in a society where men are worthy of the name, women can be enfranchised without running wild or becoming unsexed," a supporter wrote in the *Deseret Evening News*. Mormon women would never vote to abolish plural marriage, the author of the article argued, because "to do so would require repudiation of their religion" and the "disruption of many families."

When the Utah territorial legislature met in early 1870, both chambers unanimously approved the bill. On February 12, Acting Governor S. A. Mann signed the bill into law. Women in Salt Lake City voted in a municipal election just two days later. That August, they voted in a territorial election for the first time.

EMMELINE BLANCH WELLS (1828–1921)

Born in Petersham, Massachusetts, Emmeline Blanch Wells became a Mormon at fourteen and married James Harris, the son of a prominent Mormon family, at age fifteen. In 1844, the couple migrated to Mormon Church headquarters in Nauvoo, Illinois.

When their infant son died, Harris left to earn money but never returned. Emmeline became the second wife of Newel K. Whitney, and in 1848 she migrated to Utah with his family. After Whitney's death in 1850, she supported two daughters by teaching in Salt Lake City. In 1852, she became the seventh wife of Daniel H. Wells, with whom she had three daughters.

Wells was an early advocate of women's rights, having learned self-reliance through her own experiences. She was a friend of Susan B. Anthony and Elizabeth Cady Stanton. She represented Utah women in the National Women's Suffrage Association.

For 37 years, Wells was editor of the *Woman's Exponent*, a newspaper for Mormon women. A strong supporter of polygamy, she passionately defended the practice and helped ease the misunderstandings that separated Mormons and non-Mormons.

After Congress rescinded Utah women's voting rights in 1887, Wells cofounded the Woman Suffrage Association of Utah to help regain it. She lived to see the passage of the Nineteenth Amendment. Emmeline Blanch Wells died in 1921 at age ninety-three.

On the 100th anniversary of Wells' birthday, Utah women paid tribute to her by placing a bust of her likeness in the rotunda of the Utah State Capitol building. The inscription reads, "A Fine Soul Who Served Us."

TWICE THE BATTLE

From the birth of Utah Territory in 1850, Mormons had battled with Congress over polygamy and political power. The Mormons believed they had the right to govern themselves rather than be ruled by non-Mormon officials appointed by the federal government. From 1849 to 1887, Utah leaders applied for statehood six times without success.

Beginning in 1862, members of congress passed a series of anti-Mormon laws. In 1887, the Edmunds-Tucker Act finally outlawed polygamy. The practice became punishable with a heavy fine and up to five years' imprisonment. The act also dissolved the Mormon Church and allowed the federal government to confiscate all church properties valued at more than $50,000. The government also replaced local judges and took control of schools in the territory. Many laws were changed—including the

MARTHA HUGHES CANNON (1857–1932)

Martha "Mattie" Hughes Cannon was a noted physician and the first female state senator in the United States. In 1884, federal marshals arrested her new husband, Angus Cannon, for practicing polygamy. Mattie left Utah and spent two years in exile to avoid testifying against her husband. When she returned, she became active in the women's rights movement. In 1896, running against several opponents—including her husband—she won an "at large" seat in Utah's state senate—marking the first time an American woman was elected to that office. While a senator, she organized funding for speech- and hearing-impaired students, established a state board of health, and helped pass a law regulating working conditions for women. Cannon served on the Utah State Board of Health until she retired from public life and moved to California, where she died in 1932. In 1986, the Martha Hughes Cannon Health Building in Salt Lake City was dedicated in her honor. An eight-foot bronze statue of Dr. Cannon sits in the Utah Capitol Rotunda.

A daugher of Mormon leader Brigham Young played a critical role in winning back Utah women's voting rights in 1896. Susa Young Gates (1856–1933) was a writer and Mormom missionary who believed that women should be free to work or to refuse marriage if they chose. At one point, Susan B. Anthony offered Gates a leadership position in the National Women's Suffrage Association (NWSA). However, Gates could not accept the offer because she would have been required to renounce the Mormon faith.

one that allowed Utah women to vote. Any Mormon man found to be practicing polygamy was also stripped of his voting rights. About 1,300 Mormon men were arrested, tried, fined, and imprisoned. Mormons began hiding from federal law enforcers by escaping to other towns or leaving the country.

When their right to vote was rescinded in 1887, Utah women—both Mormon and non-Mormon—were outraged. Thousands of *Women's Exponent* readers protested. Leaders of the national suffrage movement agreed. Although they did not support polygamy, they believed that taking away any person's voting rights was shameful and unjust.

Emmeline Wells and other women's rights advocates formed the Woman Suffrage Association of Utah. They vowed to win back the vote. After nearly 10 years, they succeeded. In 1896, Utah achieved statehood with a constitution that guaranteed women their right to vote.

Abigail Scott Duniway (seated) signs Oregon's Equal Suffrage Proclamation on November 30, 1912, while Governor Oswald West and fellow suffragist Viola M. Coe look on. Duniway, an influential newspaper publisher, had spent about 40 years campaigning for Oregon to permit women to vote. Coe (1862–1943), a medical doctor, worked closely with Duniway on the 1911–12 campaign that resulted in woman suffrage in the state.

5

VICTORY

"Colorado passes Women's suffrage by several thousand votes," read the headlines of the *Aspen Daily Times* on November 9, 1893. Two days earlier, voters of Colorado had approved a constitutional amendment recognizing women's right to vote. It was the first state in the Union to approve women's suffrage through a popular election rather than by legislative vote.

THE BIG CAMPAIGN

The victory in Colorado was the result of a widespread campaign organized by men and women from all levels of society. "Let the women vote!" went one rallying cry, "They can't do any worse than the men have!"

Women's suffrage advocates had hoped to claim the vote in Colorado 18 years earlier, in 1875. Delegates to the constitutional convention were anxious to have the constitution ratified and approved by the end of 1876, so that Colorado could enter the Union as the "Centennial State." In their haste, they evaded controversial issues—such as women's suffrage—that might alienate voters. In the end, women's right to vote was recognized only "in all elections for district school officers and in voting upon questions relating to public schools within such district."

In the Colorado Territory during the late 1860s and early 1870s, Mary McCook, the wife of territorial governor Edward McCook, campaigned unsuccessfully for laws that would allow women to vote. Susan B. Anthony and Elizabeth Cady Stanton stayed with the McCooks while visiting Denver as part of their 1871 speaking tour of the western territories.

In January 1893, legislators introduced a bill in the House to "extend the suffrage to women of lawful age, and otherwise qualified." Legislators debated the bill at length before deciding to submit it to a popular vote.

Suffrage activists enlisted not only women's organizations, but also business leaders, labor unions, political parties, religious groups, and similar associations. They asked Governor Davis H. Waite, a reformist and former editor of the *Aspen Union Era*, to join the campaign. They handed out leaflets, delivered a series of lectures, and persuaded local newspapers to endorse their cause. The amendment passed by more than 6,000 votes.

THE HALF-CENTURY CRUSADE

Unlike the fight for women's suffrage in Colorado, the campaign in the State of Washington spanned more than 50 years. House member Arthur A. Denny introduced the bill in 1854. It failed by one vote. Not until 1867 did the issue of women's rights arise again. That year, the legislature passed a law giving the right to vote "to all white citizens above the age of 21."

In 1869, Olympia resident Mary Olney Brown, with the support of legislator Edward Eldridge, argued that because she was a white citizen older than 21, she therefore was legally entitled to vote in Washington. Although Brown did not convince legislators, she did persuade election judges in two

Washington precincts to recognize women's right to vote based on the wording of the territorial law.

Women's suffrage advocates seized upon this wording to argue their cause. They cited the language of the Fourteenth Amendment, which defines "citizen" as being "all persons born or naturalized in the United States." A group of women attempted to exercise this right at White River in 1869. Their votes were declared invalid, but 15 women successfully cast votes in a county election the following year.

In 1871, a lawyer named Daniel Bigelow introduced another bill. Abigail Scott Duniway, an Oregon campaigner for women's rights, invited Susan B. Anthony to address the legislature. Duniway had recently launched a women's rights newspaper, the *New Northwest*, and she had helped organize the Equal Rights Association in Washington Territory.

Bigelow and Anthony were eloquent in their appeal to the Washington legislature. Borrowing from Wyoming's successful argument, Bigelow sug-

THE NATIONAL AMERICAN WOMAN SUFFRAGE ASSOCIATION

The rift that developed in 1870 between the National Women's Suffrage Association and the American Women's Suffrage Association eventually healed. In 1890, the two groups combined to form the National American Woman Suffrage Association (NAWSA). NAWSA continued the work of both earlier groups. It was the parent organization for scores of local and regional women's suffrage organizations throughout the country. The largest and most important suffrage organization in the United States, NAWSA's primary goal was to push for an amendment to the U.S. Constitution that guaranteed women their right to vote. After the Nineteenth Amendment passed in 1920, NAWSA became the League of Women Voters. Today, this organization continues to work toward women's equality and voting rights.

gested that passing a women's suffrage law would have "the most gratifying of results—the immigration of a large number of good women to the Territory."

They were unsuccessful—and worse, the legislature passed a new bill clarifying the vague wording of the 1867 voting rights bill: "Hereafter no female shall have the right of ballot or vote at any poll or election precinct in this Territory, until the congress of the United States of America shall, by direct legislation upon the same, declare the same to be the supreme law of the land."

DETERMINED TO SUCCEED

Women's rights advocates refused to give up. Anthony's presence in Washington Territory had sparked the creation of several women's suffrage

ABIGAIL SCOTT DUNIWAY (1834–1915)

Abigail Scott Duniway was a nationally renowned crusader for women's suffrage. At 17, she traveled overland with her family from Illinois westward on the Oregon Trail. Duniway's mother and youngest brother died from a cholera outbreak on the trail. In Oregon, she taught school children and then married a farmer. When her husband lost money and suffered a serious accident, Duniway became a milliner to support her six children. Soon, however, she discovered that her real passion was advocating for women's rights. She began publishing the *New Northwest* in 1871. With the support of Susan B. Anthony, she became a highly respected women's rights leader. She was determined to win suffrage for women in what she called her "chosen bailiwick": Oregon, Washington, and Idaho—and ultimately she succeeded. Idaho women won the vote in 1896, Washington in 1910, and Oregon in 1912, just eight years before the Nineteenth Amendment became law.

As women in the western territories sought the right to vote, others continued the fight for suffrage on a national level. This illustration from *Frank Leslie's Illustrated Newspaper* shows Victoria Claflin Woodhull (1838–1927) addressing the Judiciary Committee of the U.S. House of Representatives in 1871. Woodhull argued that the Fourteenth and Fifteenth Amendments, which granted all citizens the right to vote, should apply to both women and men. Her widely publicized appearance made her a hero to the women's rights movement. In 1872, Woodhull would become the first female candidate for president of the United States, having been nominated by the National Radical Reformers party.

groups, and the demand grew for recognition of their civil rights.

In 1873, Edward Eldridge attempted once again to introduce a suffrage measure to the legislature. Once again it failed. Between 1875 and 1881 many new bills were introduced, but all were defeated.

In 1878, delegates to a constitutional convention excluded women's suffrage by a single vote. That same year, Washington Territory voters—all of whom were male—rejected two ballot measures on women's suffrage during a vote on the constitution.

Women did achieve small victories during this long battle. In 1877 the Territorial Legislature passed a law that permitted taxpaying women to vote in school elections. Suffragists criticized the law, however. They argued that confining women's voting rights to school elections suggested that their world should revolve around home and family alone.

REFORM AND PROHIBITION

Finally, in 1883—nearly 30 years after the first bill was introduced—both chambers of the Washington legislature passed a bill authorizing women's suffrage. Governor William Newell signed it into law on November 23, 1883. Three years later, the territorial legislature clarified the wording of the 1883 law: "All American citizens, male and female" could vote in Washington Territory.

Washington women wasted no time exercising their newly claimed right. With other voters, they elected a new reform government in Seattle and helped send a Democratic delegate to the U.S. Congress.

They were also instrumental in passing laws regarding prohibition. This concerned local activists, including Abigail Scott Duniway. Many women's suffragists were involved in the prohibition movement, and the two issues were linked in the public's mind. She believed that the best way for suffrage to remain permanent was to divorce it from the issue of prohibition in the minds of voters—especially male voters.

THE VOTE IS RESCINDED

But another problem loomed. In 1887, citing a technicality in the legislation, the Supreme Court of Washington Territory revoked women's suffrage. The legislature quickly remedied the error, but the new measure excluded women from serving on juries. Opponents of women's suffrage again took the issue to the territorial Supreme Court. In 1888, the Court ruled that the federal government had intended to place the word "male" before "citizenship" in the Washington Territory Organic Act when it established voter

Emma Smith DeVoe (1848–1927) was a talented speaker and organizer. She led campaigns that helped women gain the vote in Idaho (in 1896) and Washington (in 1910). In 1911, DeVoe founded the National Council of Women Voters, which was intended to educate women voters in the territories about important election issues and to to lobby for legislation that would extend the voting franchise to all women.

qualifications. This ruling completely rescinded women's voting rights in the territory.

The cause of suffrage in Washington Territory was seriously weakened. When the territory applied for statehood the next year, delegates to a new constitutional convention decided not to include a provision for women's suffrage.

Statehood in 1889 seemed to offer some promise to revive the women's suffrage issue. Limited suffrage for school board elections, which had been reinstated after statehood, allowed women to gain a small foothold in the long climb back to full suffrage.

Not until 1906 did a new generation of activists attempt to secure their right to vote. Emma Smith DeVoe, a professional organizer for NAWSA, and the renowned suffragist May Arkwright Hutton, led the campaign.

DeVoe, Hutton, and other organizers canvassed the state to enroll suffragists in the cause. They lobbied legislators sympathetic to their issues. They handed out almost a million pamphlets. They had enlisted the endorsement of the Washington State Grange, the labor unions, the Farmer's Union, and other influential groups. By February 1909, victory seemed to be at hand.

The ballot measure to amend the Washington constitution won by majority in November 1910. Every county in the state voted in favor. Washington had finally joined Wyoming, Utah, Colorado, and Idaho in rec-

A woman puts up a billboard encouraging Colorado women to vote against incumbent president Woodrow Wilson in the 1916 election. Alice Paul, leader of the National Woman's Party, believed that pressure from female voters would force politicians to recognize the right of all women to vote. Although Wilson was re-elected, he did change his position on suffrage during his second term.

ognizing women's right to vote. And as the first state in the 20th century to pass women's suffrage, Washington inspired a nationwide push to secure an amendment to the U.S. Constitution.

NO STOPPING NOW

Women would secure their right to vote in California in 1911, and in Oregon, Kansas, and Arizona in 1912. As its first official act, the Alaska territorial legislature approved women's suffrage that year as well. Montana and Nevada followed in 1914. South Dakota and Oklahoma recognized women's voting rights in 1918.

In 1910, the year Washington voters approved a constitutional amendment in favor of women's suffrage, the Women's Political Union held its first suffrage parade in New York City. Three years later, Alice Paul and Lucy Burns organized a suffrage parade through Washington, D.C., the day before President Woodrow Wilson's inauguration.

Between 1917 and 1919, more than 2,000 women picketed the White House. About 500 women were arrested, many on trumped-up charges of "obstructing traffic," and 168 women were imprisoned. Among them was Alice Paul, leader of the National Woman's Party. To protest the abusive treatment they received, in November 1917 Paul went on a hunger strike. In response, prison doctors transferred Paul to a psychiatric ward and force-fed her for three weeks. She refused to end the hunger strike, or her campaign for suffrage.

That same year, women's suffrage was approved in North Dakota, Ohio, Indiana, Rhode Island, Nebraska, Michigan, New York, and Arkansas.

In 1919, the Nineteenth Amendment to the Constitution, recognizing that women had the right to vote, was adopted by a joint resolution of Congress. Three-quarters of the 48 states now had to vote in support of the amendment for it to become the law of the land. On August 26, 1920, Tennessee became the 36th state to ratify the Nineteenth Amendment. Women of the United States were finally enfranchised.

LOOKING BACK... AND LOOKING AHEAD

In Seneca Falls, New York, in July 1998, First Lady Hillary Clinton addressed a large crowd gathered to celebrate the 150th anniversary of the Seneca Falls Convention. Clinton described some of the men and women who traveled to Wesleyan Chapel in 1848 for the first women's rights convention. Then she reflected on what their actions mean to us today:

> I often wonder . . . who of us—men and women—would have left our homes, our families, our work to make that journey one hundred and fifty years ago. Think about the incredible courage it must have taken to join that procession. . . .
>
> [Elizabeth Cady] Stanton was inspired, along with the others who met, to rewrite our Declaration of Independence, and they boldly asserted, "We hold these truths to be self-evident, that all men and women are created equal."
>
> "All men and all women." It was the shout heard around the world, and if we listen, we can still hear its echoes today. We can hear it in the voices of women demanding their full civil and political rights anywhere in the world. . . . We can even hear those echoes today in Seneca Falls. We come together . . . to celebrate those who met here one hundred and fifty years ago, to commemorate how far we have traveled since then, and to challenge ourselves to persevere on the journey that was begun all those many years ago.

CHAPTER NOTES

p. 10:   "I do not believe there was . . ." Judith Wellman, "Charlotte Woodward," Women's Rights National Historical Park. http://www.nps.gov/wori/historyculture/charlotte-woodward.htm.

p. 10:   "one unity with the husband" Sandra L. Myres, *Westering Women and the Frontier Experience, 1800–1915* (Albuquerque: University of New Mexico Press, 1982), pp. 213–14.

p. 12:   "grew up so thoroughly . . ." Crista DeLuzio, ed., *Women's Rights: People and Perspectives* (Santa Barbara, Calif.: ABC-CLIO, 2010), p. 59.

p. 13:   "Many who have . . ." Frederick Douglass, quoted in Elizabeth Cady Stanton, et al., *History of Woman Suffrage*, Vol. 1 (New York: Fowler & Wells, 1881), pp. 74–75.

p. 14:   "I'm afraid I'll never vote" Judith Wellman, *The Road to Seneca Falls: Elizabeth Cady Stanton and the First Women's Rights Convention* (Urbana: University of Illinois Press, 2004), p. 232.

p. 14:   "My heart is with all women . . ." Wellman, "Charlotte Woodward."

p. 17:   "ignorance, and slavish dependence" Mary Wollstonecraft, *A Vindication of the Rights of Woman: With Strictures on Political and Moral Subjects*, 3rd ed. (London: J. Johnson, 1796), p. 385.

p. 17:   "may be convenient slaves . . ." Wollstonecraft, *A Vindication*, p. x.

p. 18:   "For the interest of . . ." Hannah Crocker, quoted in Elizabeth Cady Stanton, et al., *History of Woman Suffrage* (New York: Fowler & Wells, 1881), p. 303.

p. 18:   "The women are assuming . . ." Frances Wright, *Views of Society and Manners in America* (London: Longman, Hurst, Rees, Orme, and Brown, 1821), p. 422.

p. 20:   "Health, Wealth, Serenity of mind . . ." Benjamin Rush, quoted in "Ardent Spirits: The Origins of the American Temperance Movement." http://www.librarycompany.org/ardentspirits/Temperance-medicine.html.

p. 24:   "I infused into my speech . . ." Sally G. McMillen, *Seneca Falls and the Origins of the Women's Rights Movement*, (New York: Oxford University Press, 2008), p. 77.

Suffragists speak to a crowd of men and women in San Francisco, circa 1919.

p. 24: "equality before the law, without . . ." *The Proceedings of the Women's Rights Convention Held at Worcester, October 23d & 24th, 1850* (Boston: Prentiss and Sawyer, 1851), p. 15.

p. 24: "may be dated from . . ." Elizabeth Cady Stanton, et al., *History of Woman Suffrage*, Vol. 2 (New York: Fowler & Wells, 1881), p. 428.

p. 25: "It was a thousand times . . ." Myres, *Westering Women*, p. 216.

p. 26: "According to our general understanding . . ." State of Indiana, *Report of the Debates and Proceedings of the Convention for the Revision of the Constitution of the State of Indiana*. 1850 (Reprint, Indianapolis: Wm. B. Burford Printing Co., 1935), pp. 171–2.

p. 28: "managed the farm, the shop . . ." Myres, *Westering Women*, p. 218.

p. 28:   "If all that has been said . . ." J. B. McClure, ed., *Anecdotes of Abraham Lincoln and Lincoln's Stories* (Chicago: Rhodes & McClure, 1879), p. 118.

p. 29:   "secure Equal Rights to all . . ." Library of Congress, "Call for the First Anniversary of the American Equal Rights Association," The Learning Page: Civil War and Reconstruction, 1861–1877. http://memory.loc.gov/learn///features/timeline/civilwar/freedmen/mott.html.

p. 30:   "race, color, or previous . . ." U.S. Const. amend. XV, sec. 1.

p. 36:   "the whole matter of . . ." Myres, *Westering Women*, p. 221.

p. 37:   "We have been moving . . ." Ida Husted Harper, *The Life and Work of Susan B. Anthony*, Vol. 1 (Indianapolis and Kansas City: Bowen-Merrill Co., 1899), p. 388.

p. 39:   "I believe in women . . ." Blanche Beechwood (Emmeline Blanch Wells), "Why? Ah! Why?," *The Latter Day Saints' Millennial Star* 36, no. 46 (November 17, 1874), p. 722.

p. 40:   "Our ladies can prove . . ." Myres, *Westering Women*, p. 222.

p. 40:   "to do so would require . . ." Myres, *Westering Women*, p. 222.

p. 45:   "Let the women vote!" Oregon Public Broadcasting, "Abigail Scott Duniway," Oregon Experience. http://www.opb.org/programs/oregonexperiencearchive/duniway.

p. 45:   "in all elections for district . . ." Myres, *Westering Women*, p. 224.

p. 45:   "extend the suffrage to women . . ." Myres, *Westering Women*, p. 227.

p. 46:   "to all white citizens . . ." Doris Weatherford, *Woman's Almanac 2002* (Westport, Conn.: The Oryx Press, 2002), p. 300.

p. 48:   "the most gratifying . . ." Myres, *Westering Women*, p. 225.

p. 48:   "Hereafter no female shall . . ." Hubert Howe Bancroft, *The Works of Hubert Howe Bancroft, Vol. 31, History of Washington, Idaho, and Montana 1845–1889* (San Francisco: The History Company, 1890), p. 327n.

p. 50:   "All American citizens, male and female . . ." Frank Pierce, ed., *Laws of Washington*, vol. IV (Seattle: Tribune Publishing Co., 1896), p. 319.

CHRONOLOGY

1790: The colony of New Jersey recognizes the right of "all free inhabitants" to vote; women will lose their right to vote in 1807.

1792: Mary Wollstonecraft argues for women's equality in *Vindication of the Rights of Women*.

1828: Frances "Fanny" Wright is the first woman to address an American audience composed of both men and women.

1848: The first woman's rights convention, organized by Lucretia Mott and Elizabeth Cady Stanton, is held on July 19–20 in Seneca Falls, New York.

1865: The Thirteenth Amendment to the U.S. Constitution is ratified, officially abolishing slavery in the United States.

1867: Kansas holds a state referendum on suffrage. Although it fails, it is the first ever held on women's suffrage in the United States.

1869: Wyoming territorial legislature recognizes women's voting rights.

1870: Utah Territorial legislature grants full voting rights to women. The Fifteenth Amendment to the U. S. Constitution is adopted, extending suffrage to male African Americans but not to women.

1874: The Supreme Court rules that citizenship does not necessarily give women the right to vote.

1878: A federal amendment to grant women the right to vote is introduced for the first time by Senator A. A. Sargeant of California.

1883: Washington Territorial legislature grants full voting rights to women.

1887: U.S. Congress rescinds women's suffrage in Utah. The territorial Supreme Court rescinds women's suffrage in Washington Territory.

1890: The NWSA and the AWSA merge to form the National American Woman Suffrage Association (NAWSA). Wyoming enters the Union as the first state granting full women's suffrage.

1896: Utah becomes a state, and Utah and Idaho grant full voting rights to women.

1910: Washington state referendum approves full suffrage for women.

1911: California state referendum approves full voting rights for women.

1912: Oregon, Kansas, and Arizona state referenda approve full voting rights for women.

1913: Alaska Territorial Legislature approves women's right to vote as its first official act. Illinois grants women "partial suffrage" by recognizing their right to vote only in presidential elections.

1914: Montana and Nevada approve full suffrage for women.

1915: Suffrage referendum in New York state is defeated.

1917: Members of the National Woman's Party picket the White House. Alice Paul and 96 other suffragists are arrested and jailed for "obstructing traffic." Women win the right to vote in North Dakota, Ohio, Indiana, Rhode Island, Nebraska, Michigan, New York, and Arkansas.

1918: President Wilson issues a statement supporting a federal amendment to recognize woman's suffrage.

1919: The Nineteenth Amendment to the Constitution, which guarantees women the right to vote, is adopted by a joint resolution of Congress and sent to the states for ratification.

1920: On August 26, the U.S. House of Representatives and Senate approve the Nineteenth Amendment recognizing women's right to vote. It wins the necessary two-thirds ratification from state legislatures.

GLOSSARY

abolitionist—a person who is in favor of abolishing slavery.

abstain—to refrain from voting.

boycott—to join with others in refusing to deal with a person, organization, or country, usually to express disapproval.

capacity—mental or physical ability.

cede—to give up, especially by treaty.

census—a counting of the population (as of a country, city, or town).

compromise—to settle differences by finding middle ground.

conservative—tending to be cautious or moderate.

convene—to call together in a group.

convention—a meeting of persons for a common purpose.

executor—a person named to carry out the directions in a will.

federal—national; the United States distinct from its separate states.

framers—the men who helped draw up the U.S. Constitution.

lobby—to actively influence legislation.

municipal—relating or belonging to a city, town, or village.

progressive—favoring or promoting reform.

prohibition—a law or regulation forbidding the consuming of alcoholic drink.

ratify—to approve or express consent by signing.

referendum—a legislative act that requires final approval by popular vote.

rescind—to do away with by legislative action.

resolution—a formal statement of the wishes or decision of a group.

sue—to seek justice by bringing a legal action.

suffrage—the right to vote.

temperance—the use of little or no alcoholic drink.

territory—a part of the United States not included within any state but having a separate governing body.

veto—to refuse to endorse or approve.

FURTHER READING

FOR YOUNGER READERS

Bozonelis, Helen Koutras. *A Look at the Nineteenth Amendment: Women Win the Right to Vote*. Berkeley Heights, NJ: Enslow Publishers, 2008.

Crewe, Sabrina, and Dale Anderson. *The Seneca Falls Women's Rights Convention*. Milwaukee: Gareth Stevens, 2005.

DeLuzio, Crista, ed. *Women's Rights: People and Perspectives*. Santa Barbara, Calif.: ABC-CLIO, 2010.

Hicks, Peter. *Documenting Women's Suffrage*. New York: Rosen Central, 2010.

Marsico, Katie. *Women's Right to Vote: America's Suffrage Movement*. New York: Benchmark Books, 2010.

Schenken, Suzanne O'Dea. *From Suffrage to the Senate: An Encyclopedia of American Women in Politics*. Santa Barbara, Calif.: ABC-CLIO, 1999.

FOR OLDER READERS

Beeton, Beverly. *Women Vote in the West: The Woman Suffrage Movement 1869–1896*. New York: Garland Publishing, 1986.

McMillen, Sally G. *Seneca Falls and the Origins of the Women's Rights Movement*. New York: Oxford University Press, 2008.

Mead, Rebecca. *How the Vote Was Won: Woman Suffrage in the Western United States, 1868–1914*. New York: New York University Press, 2006.

Riley, Glenda. *Women and Indians on the Frontier, 1825–1915*. Albuquerque: University of New Mexico Press, 2001.

Sheppard, Alice. *Cartooning for Suffrage*. Albuquerque: University of New Mexico Press, 1994.

Wellman, Judith. *The Road to Seneca Falls: Elizabeth Cady Stanton and the First Women's Rights Convention*. Urbana: University of Illinois Press, 2004

INTERNET RESOURCES

http://www.america.gov/women-courage.html

"Women of Courage" offers stories and photos of courageous women who challenge society to uphold freedom and human rights.

http://www.legacy98.org/

Legacy98 is an online record of the 150th Anniversary of the Women's Rights Movement, launched at the world's first Women's Rights Convention in Seneca Falls.

http://www.nps.gov/wori/index.htm

The National Park Service web site for the Women's Rights National Historical Park in Seneca Falls, NY, tells the story of the 1848 Convention.

http://www.nwhm.org/

The National Women's History Museum web site offers online exhibits, biographies, photos, and activities to learn more about U.S. women.

http://www.nwhp.org/

The National Women's History Project web site offers information, resources, and educational materials about multicultural women's history.

http://theautry.org/explore/exhibits/suffrage/index.html

The Women of the West Museum web site presents the story of women's suffrage in the Western territories and states with biographies, activities, photos, and timelines.

INDEX

Numbers in **bold italics** refer to captions.

CONTRIBUTORS

THERESE DEANGELIS has been an editor for more than twenty-five years. She has authored several books for young adults on subjects ranging from the attack on Pearl Harbor to architecture of the ancient world. *The Dust Bowl*, which she co-authored, received a New York Public Library "Books for the Teen Age" award, and she edited the award-winning JUNIOR DRUG AWARENESS series for Chelsea House Publishers. Ms. DeAngelis lives in Pennsylvania with nine funny little birds and two funny people. She votes in every election.

Senior Consulting Editor **A. PAGE HARRINGTON** is executive director of the Sewall-Belmont House and Museum, on Capitol Hill in Washington, D.C. The Sewall-Belmont House celebrates women's progress toward equality—and explores the evolving role of women and their contributions to society—through educational programs, tours, exhibits, research, and publications.

The historic National Woman's Party (NWP), a leader in the campaign for equal rights and women's suffrage, owns, maintains, and interprets the Sewall-Belmont House and Museum. One of the premier women's history sites in the country, this National Historic Landmark houses an extensive collection of suffrage banners, archives, and artifacts documenting the continuing effort by women and men of all races, religions, and backgrounds to win voting rights and equality for women under the law.

The Sewall-Belmont House and Museum and the National Woman's Party are committed to preserving the legacy of Alice Paul, founder of the NWP and author of the Equal Rights Amendment, and telling the untold stories for the benefit of scholars, current and future generations of Americans, and all the world's citizens.